FINANCIAL
LITERACY BOOT CAMP
FOR TEENS AND YOUNG ADULTS

SIX STEPS TO LIVING A LIFE OF
FINANCIAL FREEDOM

FINANCIAL LITERACY BOOT CAMP
FOR TEENS AND YOUNG ADULTS

SIX STEPS TO LIVING A LIFE OF FINANCIAL FREEDOM

BY
MICHAEL D. THOMAS

Financial Literacy Boot Camp
for Teens and Young Adults
Michael D. Thomas

All rights reserved
First Edition, 2021
Copyright © 2021 Michael D. Thomas

No part of this publication may be reproduced, stored in a retrieval system, or transmitted, in any form or by means electronic, mechanical, photocopying, or otherwise, without prior written permission of the Author.

ISBN: 978-0-578-96715-8

This book is in memory of my loving mother Bertha Thomas, who taught me how to love, how to problem solve, and how to manage money and to my dad Jerry Thomas, who taught me that I could have as much money as I had the desire and belief to acquire.

Contents

About the Author:
Why Financial Literacy is Important

Step 1
Earn a living doing what you love 1

Step 2
Banking..10

Step 3
Create a Success Plan (Budget)..16

Step 4
Be Credit Wise..25

Step 5
Start Saving and Investing Early...36

Step 6
Understanding Insurance 44

Conclusion
Understanding is Powerful! 51

About the Author:

Michael believes that understanding is liberating.

Overcoming challenges and helping others is nothing new to Michael Thomas, owner of Columbia Life & Fitness Boot Camp; it is something he has been doing his entire life. He started motivating and helping friends reach their goals as a child and has followed this path ever since. Michael began his foray into business when he was in the sixth grade and became an entrepreneur for the first time. Since then, he has amassed more than 35 years of business experience and passion for public service.

Michael was born in Helena, Arkansas, a small town next to the Mississippi Delta. Life in the Delta was hard for both his parents—as it was for most Blacks in the Deep South. Many picked cotton. The next generation chopped cotton. Neither of his parents graduated from high school.

Michael's mother was a master at making ends meet. She impressed upon him to pay his bills early so that people would trust him and give him credit. Most importantly, she said, "Always have something saved for a rainy day." His mother taught him perseverance and how to be resourceful and genuinely care for people. Her practical financial advice gave him a solid foundation to live a life free of money worries and empowered him to accomplish his dreams.

At 24 years old, Michael became a licensed Series 6 financial advisor with the Securities and Exchange Commission. Since then, he has furthered his education to create a simple blueprint for anyone, regardless of education or income to live a life of abundance and build generational wealth.

Michael has continued to grow and learn throughout his career, and he brings this diverse experience and insight to his work at Columbia Life & Fitness Boot Camp. He is a United States Army Veteran, Juvenile Corrections Officer, Recreation Specialist, Youth Sunday School Leader, Battalion Chief at the Columbia Fire Department, and Personal Trainer. He is also a certified John Maxwell speaker, trainer, and coach. Michael expertly combines his professional background with his personal experience in overcoming hardships as he guides others to live their best lives.

Michael believes that tough times and failure are part of the success process and that everyone has an area in life where they could benefit from a coach to provide support, accountability, and motivation to help them achieve their own greatness. He draws from life lessons he has learned from great leaders, his own personal failures and successes, and more than 25 years of experience and training in public service to offer powerful and liberating workshops.

Michael's goal is to give the financial tools to the next generation to become millionaires, enabling them to give back millions to their communities.

Why Financial Literacy is Important

If the pilot came up to you on an airplane and asked you to switch places with her (she would be the passenger and you would be the pilot), and your goal was to fly the plane from Columbia, SC, to Washington, DC, how would you feel? Do you think you could start the engines, successfully get the aircraft off the ground, and safely land it? Chances are you would crash the plane simply because you have not been given the tools. It is the same with money. Millions of Americans are crashing their planes every day because they don't have the tools. The next few pages will give you the tools you need to live an amazing, financially secure life.

Financial literacy is the understanding of personal money management and the ability to use tools like budgeting and investing to get the most out of your finances. Financial literacy is the foundation of your relationship with money, giving you the information needed to make informed and effective decisions that will have life-long, positive effects on your finances.

This Financial Literacy Boot Camp is designed to give you a boost in your personal understanding of finances. Covering everything from creating budgets to understanding the basics of credit and even how to protect your assets. This boot camp, like many others, is your starting point; it is designed to get you in shape, in this case, financial shape. But, like all other boot camps, you get out of it what you put into it. The tools are here for you to use.

STEP 1

Earn a living doing what you love

To find the best job that brings you satisfaction and pays well, you must get to know yourself. To find the career that you love, ask yourself the following questions:

- What do I enjoy doing?
- What comes easily to me?
- What am I willing to do for free?

Use Your Talents Often
The people that get a great deal of satisfaction from their jobs are the ones who are able to do what they love, believe they are making a difference, and consistently seek to make progress and improvements.

Do What You Love
My career included serving in the United States Army and working as a juvenile corrections officer, firefighter, licensed financial advisor, personal trainer, professional speaker, and coach. I love public service and teaching as well as encouraging and coaching others. Because I love what I do, I have never worked a day in my life. I am literally paid to have fun and am thankful I learned early on what my talents and gifts are.

Some People Get Angry at Problems; Others Find a Way to Get Rich Because of Problems

Every cent spent in this world is for a problem to be solved. When we purchase food, we are solving a physiological problem to stay alive. When we get a haircut, we are solving the problem of feeling good about ourselves and being more confident. To go to a concert, we are solving the problem of being entertained and having fun. To love the work you do and to get paid well for it you, just need to figure out what problem you enjoy solving.

Once You Know the Problem You Enjoy Solving, Get Qualified to Solve It

Examples of qualifications:

- Certified electrician
- Licensed truck driver school
- Certified Microsoft Technician
- ASE certified mechanic
- Certified personal trainer
- College graduate

Practice, Practice, Practice

The secret sauce is repetition. You will become tremendously talented at anything you do over and over again with a great attitude. Your confidence will show. People will seek you out, recruit you, and pay you well for your gifts.

Once you know what problem you enjoy solving and get qualified to solve it, simply practice with a great attitude! Knowing what you are good at and practicing with a great attitude is the key.

Take the time to get to know yourself. Say yes to most opportunities that are not negative. Take as many assessments as you can to learn more about yourself. Volunteer and seek internships. To find the career that makes you happy, you must know yourself!

Again, once you know your strengths and the problem you enjoy solving, you can enjoy a career that will pay you to have fun!

Earning Power Is All About Efficiency
One day, I was on my way to the fire station at about 7:30 a.m., and I overheard the clerk complaining about how tired he was.

He said, "I got off from my main job yesterday at 5 p.m. I went home and showered and had to be here at 10:00 p.m. When I get off in 15 minutes, I have an hour before I have to head back to my main job."

I thought to myself, he does not make enough hourly, so he has to work many hours. The situation made me sad, as ; he is not living a quality life. He doesn't have time or money set aside to enjoy life. He probably doesn't have vacation or sick pay—when he doesn't go to work, he doesn't get paid. I left thinking that the smart thing to do would be to improve his skills to get a better job and increase his hourly wage to make more money for the same amount of time.

It is possible for you to work for the same number of hours and make more money!

The person who makes $10 an hour must work double the hours to make $1,000 as the person who makes $20 an hour.

The person who makes $10 an hour must work 100 hours to make $1000.

The person who makes $20 an hour only has to work 50 hours for the same $1000.

The person who earns $500 an hour only has to work 2 hours to earn $1000.

The person who makes $1000 an hour only has to work 1 hour to earn $1000.

The difference in $10 an hour vs. $1000 an hour is huge. The person who earns $1000 an hour has 99 hours left to balance and enjoy life with. Guess who gets to decide what they are worth an hour. You! Look for ways and create a plan to consistently increase your earning power and reduce your energy and presence to earn money.

Earnings and Efficiency

Hourly Rate	Hours	Salary
$10	100	$1000
$20	50	$1000
$100	10	$1000
$500	2	$1000
$1000	1	$1000

www.columbiabootcamp.com

Earning Potential

Your lifestyle and your earning potential is decided 100% by you.

Despite its differences and challenges, America still has the greatest possibilities and opportunities in the world. Regardless of your background or current situation, you can decide exactly what you want to do and what you are worth. The following story of a hospital security guard who was inspired to become a doctor is living proof of how *you* decide what the rest of your life will look like.

This story was written by the Washington Post on August 26, 2020, and updated by Michael Thomas

Thirty-four-year-old Russell J. Ledet worked as a security guard at Baton Rouge General Medical Center. He patrolled the doctors' parking lot for four years, watching medical staff come and go and dreaming of a different life.

One day, he approached surgical resident Patrick Greiffenstein and asked if he could shadow him. To Ledet's delight, the doctor said yes.

For the next few months, Ledet spent all his free time in the operating room and visiting patients with Dr. Greiffenstein. Fast-forward seven years, and Ledet is a hospital medical student at the Louisiana hospital and in his third year at Tulane University School of Medicine.

He has swapped his old uniform for medical scrubs, and he is regularly approached and congratulated by people who recognize him from his time as a security guard.

Ledet came from humble beginnings. His mother was a nursing assistant and single parent. Money was tight, and they relied on food stamps. After college, Ledet joined the navy and was stationed in Washington, DC, where he joined the reserves. When he and his wife, Mallory, returned to Louisiana, Ledet attended Southern University and A&M College in Baton Rouge. There—on the advice of his chemistry professor—he majored in biology and chemistry. He took the security guard job to help pay the mortgage and support his wife and their new baby, Maleah.

Ledet had not contemplated being a doctor, but once he started working at the hospital as a security guard, he became fascinated and motivated by the goings-on around him—the vast complexities of patients, ailments, doctors, and medicine—from gunshot wounds to new babies being born.

Dr. Greiffenstein is now a trauma surgeon, and he praised Ledet's path to medicine as "remarkable." He wrote Ledet's letter of recommendation to medical school.

When Ledet graduated, the family moved to New York so he could attend New York University. He earned his Ph.D. in molecular oncology, and Mallory attained her psychology degree at Kean University, New Jersey.

Ledet was recognized for his research into prostate cancer, but he longed for a hands-on physician role, so he applied for medical school and gained a full scholarship to attend Tulane University, New Orleans (learning the good news just after the birth of his second child, Mahlina). For his third-year rotations, Ledet was overjoyed to be assigned to his old workplace, Baton Rouge General Medical Center— it was like coming home.

His goal now is to earn a triple board residency in pediatrics, general psychiatry, and child and adolescent psychiatry, and he plans to open a clinic for marginalized communities in New Orleans. To boost his business management skills in preparation for running his own clinic, Ledet is also working toward a MBA while in medical school. He hopes his story can be an inspiration for his children and other young people.

You are your most valuable asset! Invest in yourself! Once you decide what problem you enjoy solving, get qualified and get a job. Then, look for ways to increase your earnings.

When you get paid to do what you love, increasing your earnings will be easy because you are motivated. Working in your strength zone will allow you to do the following:

- Quickly reach your goals
- Earn more money
- Increase your happiness

- Enjoy a better quality of life
- Give meaning to the time you are working

Get Started as Soon as Possible

While in high school, test-drive what you think you know about yourself. Take the time to do the following:

- Research career opportunities and earning potential
- Get a part-time job as closely related to the career as possible
- Seek internships that will allow you to build skills
- Volunteer to get experience
- Take advantage of job-shadow experiences
- Take advantage of classes available in high school or online

Once you get your first job, look for opportunities to keep learning and growing. Seek opportunities to fix problems and fill gaps that will help the organization save money, make more money, or be more efficient.

Promotion Time

Promotions are more accessible than most think. Do the following, and you will not have any competition. Often, employers already know who will get the job before it is posted.

- Be reliable
- Be on time
- Work hard
- Be a team player
- Communicate well in writing and verbally
- Have a great attitude
- Be easy to supervise
- Do what is required for the next step

Sometimes, you will be overlooked for a promotion you feel you should have received. Sometimes, others do not see us the way we see ourselves, and their view maybe more accurate. Sometimes, we are not as good as we think, or we do a poor job in one critical area, and we need to be honest with ourselves about it. Then there are times when there is a better opportunity for us. And sometimes, we are being treated unfairly. My good friend Carla Kaiser told me her father would say, "Life is fair because it is, at times, unfair to everybody." I found that to be excellent advice.

Think Long Term
Take the time to map out your next steps.

Practice. It takes approximately 10 years and 10,000 hours to master your craft.

Go Specialized
After you master your craft, everything will be easier, and your decisions will be better. Look for the area you love most about your job and work to specialize in that role. Doing what you love will dramatically increase your value in the marketplace and dramatically improve your earnings. The brain surgeon or cardiologist makes substantially more money than the family doctor.

Get a Mentor or Coach
It has been said that mentors press decades into days. The best way to learn is to find someone who has done what you want to do and ask him to share his recipe for success. A mentor or coach can give your craft a good recipe for success and improve your earnings.

Summary
- Find what you love doing
- Get qualified
- Practice until you can do it with your eyes closed
- Go specialized
- Get a mentor or hire a coach

Another Way to Get More Money

Plug the leaks! One of the easiest ways to give yourself a raise is to study your spending and stop overdoing it. Stop wasting money on stuff that does not have real value. You can have too much of a good thing. The additional $50 to $100 could make a tremendous difference in an investment account or go toward a family vacation or be given to someone in need. So, while we search for ways to improve our earning power, let's give ourselves a raise by being intentional with and mindful of our current income.

Closing

Money is everywhere. You are only limited by your desire and imagination!

STEP 2

Banking

Who Needs Them and Why?
It is extremely difficult to live in America without establishing a relationship with a bank or credit union.

Banks serve many functions. Fortunately, the purpose of banks is not a secret. The information below will help shed some light on their primary purpose and benefits, as well as the different kinds of banks you can choose from.

When we make money, there are many places we can keep it. Having loose cash at home is susceptible to theft or damage. Imagine if something terrible happened, like a house fire. You'd be busy getting your family out while your fortune went up in flames.

The number one thing that banks provide is safety for your money. For every bank that you have an account with, the FDIC (Federal Deposit Insurance Corporation) insures up to $250,000. This means that no matter what happens to the bank, or their investments, the federal government will reimburse you everything in your account, up to $250,000. That is a significant amount of money that can be kept safe and help set your mind at ease, knowing your hard-earned money is safe. If you have more than $250,000 in your account, there are other supplemental insurance policies that you can purchase to protect it, which are still cheap and more secure than stuffing it under your mattress.

That's not all banks do; they also help you get paid! Yes, that's right, they help the money get from your employer's pocket into yours. It is rare to be paid in cash these days, so most employers will write you a check. There are typically only two ways to cash that check. The first is to go to your employer's bank and cash it there. They will verify there are enough funds in your employer's account and then give you the cash. Or, if you have your own bank account, you can go to your bank, where they will cash the check, either depositing it into your account or giving you the cash in your hand.

But wait, there's more! If you have a checking account, you can sign up for direct deposit, which means having your paycheck deposited directly into your bank. This means you do not have to go to the bank to get paid, and in most cases, you get paid a day or two earlier than getting a paper check.

Banks also offer savings accounts, where they will pay you interest every single month depending on how much money is in your savings account. That's free money. Having a personal relationship with a bank can also help you secure loans, whether it be for a new house, a car, or even a personal loan. This is just a brief snapshot of what banks can do for their customers; as your relationship grows with your bank, the more they will do for you.

Now that you know you need a bank account, it's time to decide what bank you want to use. There are many kinds of banks, but they break down into three main kinds. The first are the large international banks with many locations and millions of dollars in deposits. These banks are often the easiest to open accounts with and will offer many benefits. But it is also hard to develop that relationship; they have so many customers that when you apply for a loan, they will simply approve or deny it based on the numbers. The second kind of bank is your local bank. They are similar to the large banks but may only have a few locations, and you probably know who the bank president is. These smaller banks make it easier to develop that personal relationship, which can help secure loans or other things you may need. The third kind of bank is a credit union. What makes these banks different is that the members are also part-owners of the bank. This means that you can develop an even closer relationship with the bank, but they are a little more selective on loans because they want to protect their investments closely.

Now that you understand the primary purpose of banks, some of their benefits, and the different kinds, it is time to choose the right bank for you. It is vital that you do your own research on the banks available to you. They do not have all the same benefits and may offer different fees and different rates on loans and investments. It is well worth the time to find the right bank for you to make sure you can reap the benefits. Having the right bank will help get your finances organized and keep them organized, which is essential in maintaining your financial freedom.

Selecting a Bank
With that said, let's talk about what to look out for when selecting a bank account.

First, let us consider the fees. Annually, banks make hundreds of millions of dollars on fees they charge customers to access their services. Some of these fees are listed below:

- Monthly service fee
- Minimal umaccount balance fee
- ATM fees
- Insufficient funds fees
- Overdraft protection fees

Choose a bank that does not charge monthly maintenance fees with a large network of ATMs or one that does not charge an out-of-network ATM fee and has a lenient overdraft protection fee.

Many banks offer free checking accounts and do not have minimum balance requirements. Also, some online banks do not have an out-of-the-network ATM fee.

Non-sufficient Funds
A non-sufficient funds (NSF) fee is charged when you do not have the funds in the bank to cover the cost of the item you would like to purchase and the transaction is denied

Listed below is an example of someone whose funds were in the negative and they deposited $400.00. Seven non-sufficient fund charges reduced the deposit by half.

NON-SUFFICIENT FUNDS

10/05	ATM	400.00	421.97
10/05	Non Sufficient Funds Charge	-33.00	388.97
10/05	Non Sufficient Funds Charge	-33.00	355.97
10/05	Non Sufficient Funds Charge	-33.00	322.97
10/05	Non Sufficient Funds Charge	-33.00	289.97
10/05	Non Sufficient Funds Charge	-33.00	256.97
10/05	Non Sufficient Funds Charge	-33.00	223.97
10/05	Non Sufficient Funds Charge	-33.00	190.97

Overdraft Protection
If you do not have enough money in your checking account, checks will still clear, and ATM and debit card transactions will still go through. Overdraft protection fees can be high. Some banks charge one fee per day. Others charge a fee for every transaction where the funds were not available.

Be careful and check your checking account and balances often to avoid fees for insufficient funds and overdraft protection. Some banks charge as much as $35 for each of these fees. If you are not careful, you can easily rack up $300 in charges in just a couple of days. I once had a friend forget about her annual prime fee that was set up to renew automatically. The $120 was withdrawn without her knowledge, and she used her debit card six times in a couple of days for small transactions. She was charged $35 in overdraft protection for each of the debit transactions, which racked up $210 of overdraft protection fees before she figured it out.

These fees can be devastating, especially since you already have a money shortage.

The Difference in Overdraft and Nnon-sufficient Funds
Overdrafts allow the purchase to take place when there is a shortage of funds and charges you a fee for the privilege

Non-sufficient Funds is when your purchase is declined, and you still have to pay a fee.

Checking Account
A checking account is used for day-to-day banking, including depositing your paycheck, withdrawing cash, and paying bills. It offers multiple ways to access your money—such as debit cards, ATMs, and personal checks.

At the heart of your financial life is a banking account. A checking account is the center of your operations. Very few days will go by where you don't use your debit card, write a check, use the ATM, pay a bill, or make a deposit with your checking account.

Using a check or debit card has real benefits over cash.

The benefits of a check or debit card:
- Offers protection when it's lost or stolen
- Offers proof of payment
- Easy to mail or make payments online
- Direct deposits
- Set up automatic bill payments
- Ease of tracking

Savings Accounts

Your savings account is not a checking account. Your savings account should be used as a place to save money for emergencies and short-term goals, such as vacations or a down payment. Many banks will limit your withdrawals from your savings account to six per month. If you need to access it more often than that, you need to move the money over to your checking account.

Money Market Account

Like savings accounts, money market accounts limit your number of monthly transactions, and they hold cash that you do not need right away.

Certificate of Deposit (CD)

A certificate of deposit, or CD, is a timed deposit. You promise to leave your money with the bank for a set term—typically, from a few months to five years—and in return, the bank offers higher interest rates. The longer the term, the higher the rate.

Closing

The key is to figure out what you need from a bank and select one that will not rob you for every mistake you make and kill you with fees.

STEP 3

Create a Success Plan (Budget)

Budgeting: It is unavoidable. You have to spend some of the money you make. You need food and shelter to survive and some entertainment to keep from going a little crazy. But it is also important that you do not let your spending get out of control. Sometimes you purchase items you do not need or spend more on a product when other financially responsible varieties are available. This is why it is so important to budget your monthly expenses. There are some things that you have little control over—your rent or mortgage payments need to be paid in full every month—but there are other places you can make sure you are spending responsibly. Setting a budget on how much you plan to spend on groceries or entertainment can keep you from spending more than you originally planned. The primary reason you want to budget is to keep your spending as low as possible while still being able to enjoy your life.

Conscience Spending!

It is about knowing yourself well enough to know what is important to you. It is saying yes to what you want and no to everything else. When you know what you want, peer pressure and outside influences have little effect. Life is short, and we have a limited amount of time, energy, and money. Know what you really want and say no to everything else.

There is always a trade-off taking place. The time and dollar can only be used once. Ask yourself: By saying yes to this, what am I saying no to? Let's be sure we are saying no to the things that matter the least and yes to the most important stuff.

Time is your greatest asset because it is not renewable. Once it is gone, it is gone. Use it wisely. Health is difficult to restore once it has been compromised. Time with poor health is hell. Relationships are what we live for. We all desire connection with people who are important to us. Be careful not to allow more money to *reduce* time, health, and relationships!

Tell Your Money What to Do!
First-generation college students will often earn four to five times more money than their parents. But without financial literacy and the tools to manage it, they will suffer the same financial stress as their parents. In fact, their financial stress may be worse than their parent's because their ability to earn more means they may have more desires, spend more, and end up with more debt.

Money is Everywhere in Abundance
You can create whatever lifestyle you desire as long as you have the belief and the tools to support it.

Money is a Tool to Live and Enjoy Life!
To get a better understanding of money and its uses, I worked hard to simply learn how it can be used. Once we understand how it can be used, we can create a success plan based on the important ways to use it.

Five ways to use money:
- Take care of living expenses
- Save for future goals
- Enjoy it and have fun

- Give some away
- Invest to make more money

If you want to have it all and not make any sacrifices, you just have to figure out how to make a lot of money.

If retiring early is a priority, create a budget to set aside as much of your income as possible in investments and reduce other areas of your spending.

If owning a nice home and car is important, you make the funds available to do so.

If enjoying life and shopping is important, then you work to reduce your living expenses to make sure you can fully enjoy these areas regularly.

Listed below is The Success Plan for a more balanced approach.

What is an Emergency Fund?
An emergency fund is a bank account with money set aside to pay for large, unexpected expenses, such as, medical expenses, home repairs, car repairs, and unemployment.

Why Do I Need an Emergency Fund?
Emergency funds create a financial buffer that can keep you afloat in a time of need without having to rely on credit cards or high-interest loans. It can be imperative to have an emergency fund if you have debt because it can help you avoid borrowing more.

To reduce the stress of unforeseen emergencies, save six to nine months of your monthly cost of living.

Recently in the middle of one of the coldest winters, my heater died. The cost was $5200 to replace it. If I did not have the money saved for these types of unexpected problems or a good credit score to borrow the money, I would have had a real crisis on my hands.

Create a Winning Formula
In the book, "I Will Teach You to Be Rich," the author Ramit Sethi lays out four categories of spending:

1. Fixed cost: 50-60%
2. Investment: 10%
3. Savings goals: 5-10%
4. Guilt-free spending: 20-35%

The Success Plan
Listed below are the changes that I made to my plan. Feel free to make changes to create a winning formula based on what is important to you.

Lay a Rock-Solid Foundation
Out of the gate, move to the front of the line and pay yourself 10-20% of your income. Following this simple rule will create a foundation to live a life of financial freedom. Get this right and you will be set for life!

Keep Living Expenses Low Enough to Have an Enjoyable Life
You must first create the ability to earn enough money so that your living expenses make up less than 55% of your income. When your living expenses take up 75-80% of your income, you will not have enough money to do the things that make life fun.

Fund your Short-term Goals
Save 5% for short-term goals, such as a vacation or purchasing a home. Short-term goals give us something to look forward to and make life exciting!

Have Fun and Enjoy Life
Set aside 20-25% to shop and have fun by going to the movies, restaurants, concerts, and football games. These are things that make

daily life worth living. When your living expenses are too high, you will find yourself working daily without the financial bandwidth that makes life fun. The lower you keep your living expenses, the more you will have to enjoy life.

Give Some Away
Be sure to set aside money to give away. With the last 10%, give to a cause in your heart or assign it to another area of your plan.

In the next chapter, I will give you some understanding of how to invest the first 10% to make money while you sleep.

Knowing what you want will allow you to create a success plan, sometimes called a budget. Knowing what we want allows us to say yes to the things we want the most and easily see what distracts us from our goals.

Work to live within your current financial means. Having more desires than you can afford is a recipe for financial disaster. Remember that your current income is temporary and can be increased as often as you want for as much as you want.

The 20-25% Set Aside for Fun and Entertaining Makes Life Worth Living
Imagine having only just enough to pay the bills. Or worse, the financial stress of not having enough to cover your bills. Who wants to live long portions of their lives this way? It is important to have money set aside just to have fun and enjoy life. For all of us, fun and entertainment are different. Listed below are a few ideas:

- Traveling
- Shopping
- Dining
- Exercising

- Giving
- Concerts
- Festivals
- Movies
- Adventures
- Hosting friends and family

I enjoy mountain biking, kayaking, camping, concerts, reading, coffee shops, traveling, meals, and conversations with friends and family.

Many of the things I enjoy, such as biking and kayaking, have an upfront cost to purchase equipment but require little more to enjoy regularly. It is important to have some hobbies that have little cost and energy associated with them so you can sprinkle in more expensive joys and stay within budget. For instance, if you enjoy traveling, you may be surprised by the beautiful day or overnight trips you can easily drive to from your home.

Again, you will need 20-25% of your income to make life worth living. The best way to do this is to keep living expenses below 565%. You can do this by not paying more for a house or car than you can afford.

Keep Student Loan and Credit Card Debt as Low as Possible
Lastly, be sure not to let past debts rob you of your future.

Work to keep student loans and credit card debt as low as possible, so they don't keep you from purchasing a home, going on vacation, or going to a concert.

Setting a Budget
Before you can set a budget, you have to pay taxes and pre-tax employee benefits. Then you create a spending plan based on what is left.

Where is My Money

When you see your first paycheck, you might think, where is the rest of my money? There is a difference between what you earned and what you get to take home.

Gross pay is the amount you are paid before taxes and pre-tax deductions.

Net Pay is the amount you are paid after taxes and pretax deductions.

The difference between your gross pay and the net pay that you take home is the amount you have to pay for federal taxes, state taxes, social security, Medicare, and some pre-tax deductions.

Federal taxes are used to fund the military and programs like Federal Aviation Administration.

Social security is a federal insurance program designed to help Americans during retirement.

Medicare is a federal health insurance for people 65 and over.

State taxes are used to help fund things like schools and state parks.

In addition to paying taxes, you may have other pre-tax deductions that come out of your gross pay.

What are Pre-tax Deductions?

A pre-tax deduction is money subtracted from your wages before the money is withheld for taxes, lowering your taxable income. Pre-tax deductions are usually your employee benefits. Not all benefits are pre-tax deductions.

How Pre-tax Deductions Impact Taxes

Example
Let's say that your pre-tax deduction is $100 and your gross pay is $1000.

First, subtract the $100 pre-tax withholding from your gross pay ($1,000):

$1,000 – $100 = $900

The employee's taxable income is $900 for the pay period. You can now withhold taxes based on $900 rather than $1,000.

Listed below is a real example of taxes and pre-tax deductions.

Annual salary $50,899
Gross pay semi – monthly $2,121

Taxes		FICA		Pre-Tax	
Federal	$183	Social security	$118	$401K	$150
State	$90	Medicare	$28	Medical	$120
Local	$00			Dental	$15
				Vision	$35
				HSA	$50
Total	$273.00		$146		$370
Deductions	$789				

Net pay semi-monthly income: $1,333

Net pay Semi-monthly Income: $1,333 X 2 +$2,666

What are you willing to go without to make up the difference? If you choose not to go without anything, remember you live in an abundant country and money is everywhere!

Salaries & Budgets

Annual salary $50,899

Gross	$5332		
Net Income	$2666		
Fed Taxes	$183	House	$1100
State Taxes	$90	Light & gas	$150
Social Sec	$118	Water & sewer	$120
Medicare	$28	Cable & internet	$120
Total	$419	Cell phone	$100
		Grocery	$300
401K	$150	Car note	$400
Medical	$120	Car insurance	$150
Dental	$15	Fuel	$200
Vision	$35	Student loan	$300
HAS	$50	Credit card	$100
		Grocery	$300
Pre-Tax Total	$370	Fun & entertainment	$350
		Lunch	$150
Total Deductions	$789 X2 $1578	Total Expenses	$3840
		Difference	$1174

Annual salary $75,000

Gross	$6250		
Net Income	$3954		
Fed Taxes	$396	House	$1100
State Taxes	$160	Light & gas	$150
Social Sec	$180	Water & sewer	$120
Medicare	$42	Cable & internet	$120
Total	$778	Cell phone	$100
		Grocery	$300
401K	$150	Car note	$400
Medical	$120	Car insurance	$150
Dental	$15	Fuel	$200
Vision	$35	Student loan	$300
HAS	$50	Credit card	$100
		Grocery	$300
Pre-Tax Total	$370	Fun & entertainment	$350
		Lunch	$150
Total Deductions	$1148 X2 $2296	Total Expenses	$3840
		Difference	$114

STEP 4

Be Credit Wise

What is Credit?

We live in an increasingly digital world, which is especially true for our finances. While it is great to have access to our money 24 hours a day, seven days a week, it also comes with some dangerous pitfalls. With the rise of digital finances, there has been a marked decrease in understanding credit, credit scores, and their importance. This lack of understanding can lead to overspending, out-of-control debt, and more.

Let's take a look at what credit actually is in its simplest form. When you go to a store and make a purchase with cash, you are completing a transaction. The owner of the store gets your cash, and you get the product you purchased. But sometimes, you don't have enough cash on hand and need that product right now. In the past, the store owner would give you credit, allowing you to pay them for the product at a later date, while taking the product home that day. This type of credit often did not involve interest rates or payments; it was more of a gentleman's agreement.

Later, there was a rise in companies that work as middlemen in offering credit. The most common of these are credit card companies.

Today, you go into the store to buy the product, but instead of the owner giving you credit, you swipe your credit card. You still get to go home with the product, but now the owner gets paid by the credit card company. Instead of having to pay the owner, you now have to pay back the credit card company. But the credit card company needs to make money as well, so it charges you interest, late fees, processing fees, etc.

But there's a further complication to all of this. How does the credit card company know that you will pay off the credit they have extended to you? In the past, the owner of the store likely knew who you were, knew your family, where you lived. Because they knew you, they knew that they could trust you to pay off the credit they had extended. This need to know a person is what gave rise to the credit score.

Your credit score is a numerical number, assigned in a range between 300 to 850. They use many factors to determine your score—how much debt you have, how often you make payments on your debt, how long you have had each debt, and more. At the end of the day, when creditors look at your score, the higher your score the more likely they are to extend you new credit or increase the amount of credit extended to you.

In the past, people would often save up for large purchases like cars or homes. Even if they could not afford them, there were methods that would allow them to purchase over time. In fact, Sears used to sell houses through catalogs. You would purchase different pieces of the home, and it would come with instructions for you to build it on your own. But today, very few people can make these large purchases with cash outright. They need credit.

This modern need for credit is why it is so important to keep track of your credit score. Sometimes there may be a mistake that has a negative effect on your credit. In that case, it is your responsibility to contest it and have the mistake removed. Other times, you might make a mistake and forget a payment or a bill. That missed payment will have an effect on your credit report, and checking it can help you realize your mistake and correct it before it has a long-term effect on your score. The best place to check your credit score is at one of the three credit score companies, Experian, Transunion, and Equifax. Each of these companies has its own website to create an account, verify your identity, and check your current credit score.

Credit

There are three major credit bureaus. They all have subtle differences in calculating credit scores. Credit card companies, banks, and other institutions usually use the middle score as a determining factor to make a decision. Listed below are three credit scores from the major bureaus.

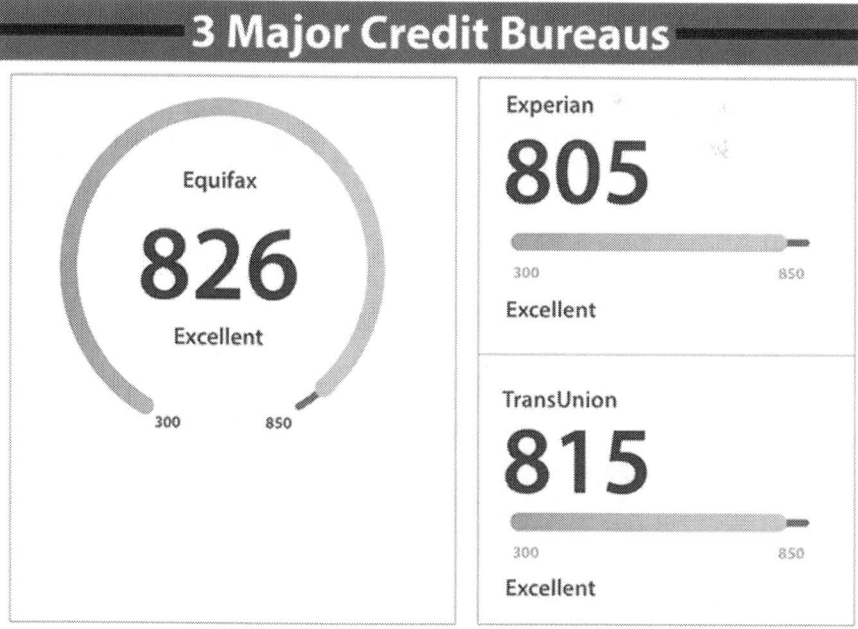

Maintain your credit so you can get approved for a place to stay and not have to put down large deposits for electricity, water, and other utilities! A good credit score will make the difference as to whether you can purchase a car, get a low-interest rate on a loan, or get an offer for certain jobs.

Your credit score is used to determine how risky it is to loan money to you. As you can see on the chart below, anything less than a 650 is high risk, and most lenders will not approve a loan or credit card for you. It will be almost impossible to get approved for a mortgage and very difficult to rent an apartment. Such a low score screams that you have money problems and find it difficult to pay debts. Low credit scores push financial dreams out of reach and raise the cost of living tremendously because of

the additional costs associated with higher interest rates, deposits for utilities, or managing rent-to-own situations.

Credit Scores Range from 300-850

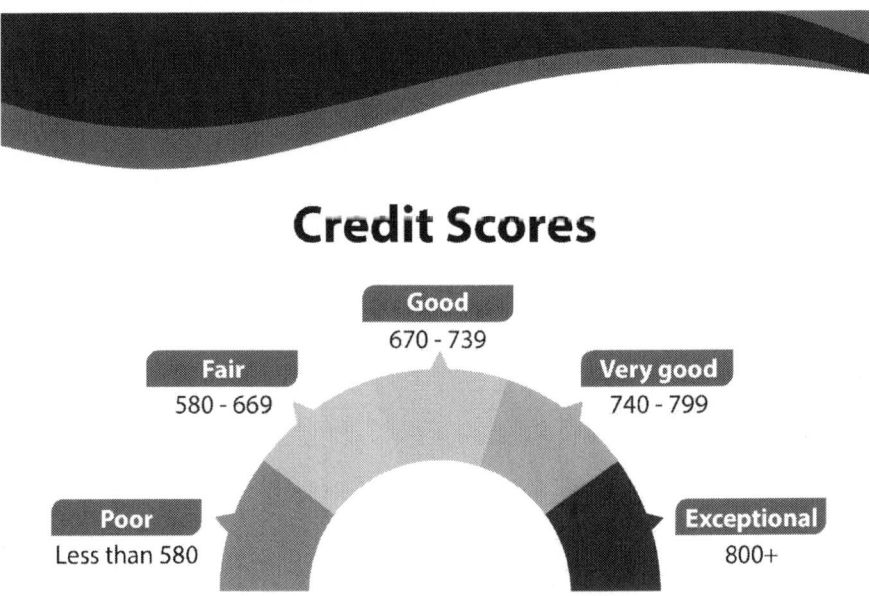

Your credit score will often determine the quality of your life—whether life is fun or stressful. I mean, who wants to get up every day to go to work and just pay the bills and not have any fun?

The difference between a 560 and a 680-credit score could be between $1,000 and $1,500 per month. That extra cash could go a long way to accomplishing financial dreams and short-term goals.

How Your Credit Score is Generated

Let's talk about how to get a great credit score. The diagram below shows us how a credit score is formulated.

As you can see, the amount you owe and your payment history make up a whopping 65% of the credit formula.

How to Establish Credit

Out of the gate as an 18 year-old, you will be given a chance to establish your credit. You will probably be given a credit score of between 620 and 640. Let's say you apply for a credit card and get a $500 limit.

If you keep the balance below 30% and make the payments on time for 12 months, your credit score could rise to about 680, which is a fair credit score.

On the other hand, let's say you get a $500 limit and charge $400 on the card, which gets you above 30% of the credit limit, and you make one 30 day late payment in 12 months, this could cause your score to drop to 500—putting you in place to be denied a car loan or anything else without a cosigner.

One 30 day late payment can cause your credit score to drop 100 points. A 60 day late payment will have even more of an impact. If you cannot do anything else, make a minimum payment. If the minimum payment is too high, call and ask for a lower minimum until you can get things back on track.

New credit usually causes a slight drop in your credit score until the credit bureaus can see how you are handling the new payment.

Credit Mix
- One major credit card
- One fixed loan, such as a car note or mortgage
- Pay on time and keep balances below 30%

And, as the years go by, having a long history of making payments on time and keeping balances low will ensure your credit score continues to rise.

New Credit
New credit usually causes a slight drop in your credit score until the credit bureaus can see how you are handling the new payment.

How to Earn an Excellent Credit Score:
- Make payments on time
- Keep your balance below 30% of your credit limit

- Get one major credit card and one fixed loan from the bank—a car note or mortgage
- The longer you do the above three, the better your credit score will be

Cosigning

Cosigning is a serious business and could have devastating consequences for the cosigner. Sometimes, people have good reasons for not being able to pay their bills on time, such as health problems or job loss. Most often, people just do not pay their loans and credit cards as promised. You will not be any different. If you cosign, you are promising to pay that loan back if the person you are cosigning with does not pay. If you don't make the payments, your credit will be negatively affected as well.

Do not let anyone convince you to buy things with your credit. Your credit is the gatekeeper for large, important purchases, such as buying a home or car or getting a business loan.

And as we talked about earlier, when you get over your head in debt, you steal from the 10–20% of your budget that makes life fun. It has been said that when you borrow, you borrow from two people;the lender and your future self! Debt racked up years ago will force us to say no to many things we would like to do today.

Principal

"In the context of borrowing, principal is the initial size of a loan; it can also be the amount still owed on a loan."

The amount of interest you pay on a loan is determined by the principal. For instance, if your loan has a principal amount of $10,000 and an annual interest rate of 5%, you will have to pay $500 in interest for every year the loan is outstanding." Investopedia

Interest (APR)

What Is an Annual Percentage Rate (APR)?
"The term "annual percentage rate (APR) refers to the annual rate of interest charged to borrowers and paid to investors. APR is expressed as a percentage that represents the actual yearly cost of funds over the term of a loan or income earned on an investment. This includes any fees or additional costs associated with the transaction, but it does not take compounding into account. The APR provides consumers with a bottom-line number they can easily compare with rates from other lenders." Investopedia

The illustration below is the cost of borrowing $9500 at an 11% interest rate. How would you like to make $90 per month of passive income?

The Cost of Interest

05/15/2021	PRINCIPAL $217.18
05/15/2021	INTEREST $90.17
04/15/2021	PRINCIPAL $212.15
04/15/2021	INTEREST $95.20
03/15/2021	PRINCIPAL $219.48
03/15/2021	INTEREST $87.87
02/15/2021	PRINCIPAL $208.09
02/15/2021	INTEREST $99.26
01/15/2021	PRINCIPAL $206.13
01/15/2021	INTEREST $101.22
12/15/2020	PRINCIPAL $207.48
12/15/2020	INTEREST $99.87

Monitor Your Credit Report

Listed below is a copy of a sample credit report. Please take the time to review and understand all that is on the report. Your credit report should be 100% accurate. Anything that is not accurate on the credit report can be disputed. Once you file a dispute, the credit reporting agency must start an investigation to make the proper adjustments.

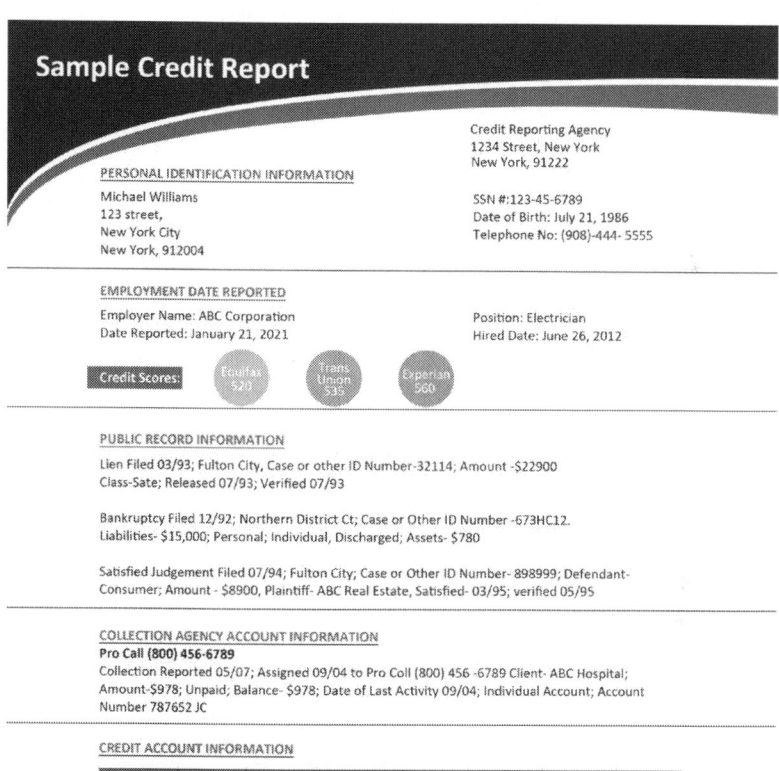

You are allowed one free credit report per year, or you can pay for credit monitoring that will alert you by text or email of any new attempts to open lines of credit or suspicious activity. Most subscriptions offer fraud and identity protection as well.

The Cost of Credit
- The cost of credit will depend on the interest rate, how much you borrow, and how long you take to pay it back.

Listed below are examples of the different costs associated with six mortgages. The costs vary based on how much you borrow (principal), the interest rate, and the term of the mortgage (how long it takes you to pay it back).

The first two have the same amount borrowed and the same interest rate but different terms (number of years to pay it back). On the 15-year mortgage, you save $73,768 in interest.

The 3rd and 4th have higher interest rates than the 1st and 2nd.

The 5th and 6th have higher principles.

Take the time to understand that how much you pay for your mortgage is based on how much you borrow, the interest rate you are able to get, and the length of your term.

The Cost of Credit

Principle	$165,000	$165,000	$165,000	$165,000	$200,000	$200,000
Years	30	15	30	15	30	15
Interest %	4.5	4.5	6	6	6	6
Monthly payment	$836.03	$1262.24	$989.26	$1392.36	$1199.10	$1687.71
Total interest	$135,971	$62,203.01	$191,133.01	$85,625.48	$231,676.38	$103,788.46
Total payment	$300,971	$227,203.01	$356,133.01	$250,625.48	$431,676.38	$303,788.45

Closing

In closing, it is important to note that this is a simplified explanation of what credit and credit scores are. Credit is extended to allow you to pay later for products that you receive now. Your credit score is like a grade that shows how trustworthy you are to have credit extended to you. This brief article is a jumping-off point, giving you the basics as you continue to educate yourself more. Remember, the goal is to make sure you understand how credit works.

STEP 5

Start Saving and Investing Early

There is a very popular saying that you have most likely heard before, 'Make your money work for you.' The best way to make your money work for you is by investing it, earning interest and dividends. One of the most common methods of investing is to purchase stocks in the stock market. Note, no investment is 100% safe, but there are many ways to mitigate the risks, sometimes even making them negligible.

Saving and Investing in Your 20s Is Important and Has Huge Financial Consequences
Most people wait until their 30s to start saving and investing. The difference between investing in your 20s and your 30s because of the lost power of regular contributions and compound interest those years make could easily be $700,000 by the time you are 65 years of age. Regular investments, time, and compound interest is a winning formula to make you a millionaire. The key is getting started early. Your older self will thank you for being smart if you start saving and investing in your 20s.

Secure a Financial Advisor
Secure a reputable financial advisor as soon as you can. Many people think they need a lot of money to get a financial advisor. The exact

opposite is true. You will probably need a financial advisor to *get* a lot of money. Ask people that you know and trust for recommendations for a great financial advisor.

Passive Income

I often ask students, at what age did someone tell you that you do not have to work for money? Almost always, the answer is never. I also did not know there was a huge population of people getting paid a lot of money while they were sleeping or on vacation. These investors learned to use the power of a dollar to make another dollar. They learned the power of investing in the stock market or in real estate to make passive income, sometimes with other people's money. "Money is always working, and it never sleeps." "Money is a 24-7 employee." The trick is to keep some and make it work.

Earned Income

I was taught as a child to go to work and earn money. The problem with earned money is that it requires energy and for you to be present. When you clock out, the money stops. Earned income is important; it is the foundation a person needs to build wealth and a portion of it is needed to cover living expenses. The most important part of earned income is the 10-20% you keep to invest for making more money.

The trick is to get started early. When you get any money, regardless of how small it is, save 10%. Open a savings account and save 10% so your money can start making money. The money that your money makes is called interest. Interest is good. Compound interest is a beast. Albert Einstein said compound interest is the eighth wonder of the world.

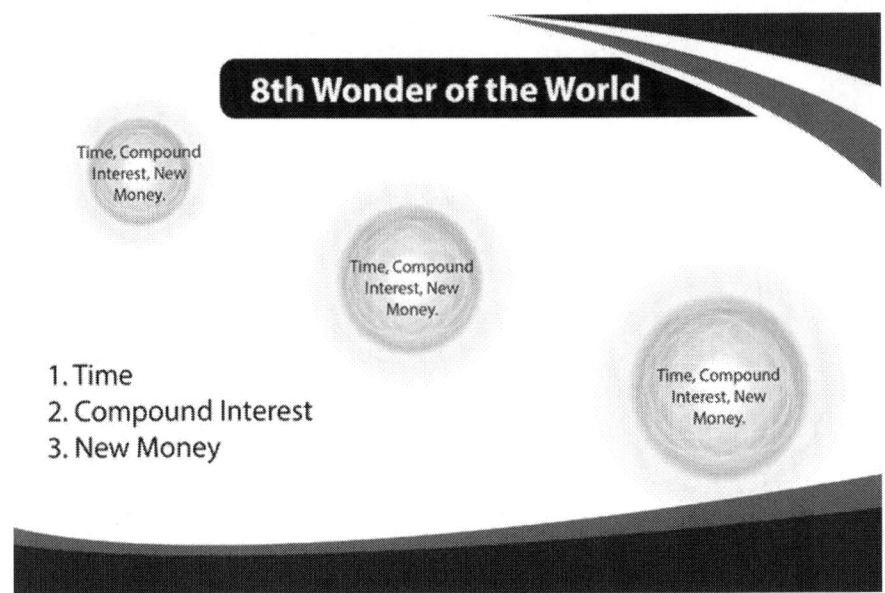

1. Time
2. Compound Interest
3. New Money

Compound Interest

Compounding interest is "the addition of interest to the principal sum of a loan or deposit. Ok, so your next question is probably what does that mean? Essentially, when you invest money, you will earn a certain percentage of interest on that money. When that interest is added to the original investment, you can earn interest on that money as well." Wikipedia

Why Does the Bank Pay You to Keep Your Money Safe?

Because when you put your money in the bank, it does not stay in the bank. The money that you deposit into your savings account is loaned to people who are borrowing money from the bank to buy the things that they want. They may charge the borrower 10% interest and may pay you 2% interest for the use of your money.

Now, let's move from saving and getting a very small amount of interest to becoming the lender and getting a bigger return.

Bonds

You can use the 10% you pay yourself to earn more money while you sleep by adding bonds to your investment portfolio.

What is a bond? A bond is an investment where the investor loans money to the government and corporations. Your country needs money to build bridges and develop technology. The same is true for states and corporations that need money to build new schools and parks and to grow their businesses. You can purchase US Treasury bonds starting at $25 and the bond issuer will pay you interest on that money you loaned them.

Stocks

Let's look at how the stock market works. When you purchase stock, you are purchasing a small part of the company; you are technically one of many owners. The more stock you own in a company, the more control you have over the company. As a first-time investor, you will not be taking control of any companies, but you can earn a piece of their profits.

Companies sometimes need money to grow their business. One way to raise money is to sell shares in a company to the public. For example, if it was my goal to open 100 Columbia Life and Fitness Boot Camps nationwide, I would have to raise money to lease buildings, purchase equipment, and hire staff. To raise this money I could float a bond, which is a loan that I would have to pay back with interest. Or I could sell stock shares of my company to investors. The investors could buy as much as they wanted or could afford. The company is then responsible for doing the work to get the largest return for its shareholders. When investors purchase stock in companies, such as Nike, they have some of the smartest and most talented people in the world working as lawyers, marketers, designers, and accountants to get the product to market as cheaply as possible and for the largest profit possible. As a result, based on the number of shares they own, investors are sent a dividend check for the earnings on their portion of stocks. It's called a dividend because it is their divided portion.

How much work did the investor do for this check? The answer is none. This is what is called passive income. Passive income is when money earns money.

Mutual Funds

A mutual fund is a company that brings together money from many people and invests it in stocks, bonds, or other assets. The combined holdings of stocks, bonds, or other assets the fund owns are known as its portfolio. Each investor in the fund owns shares, which represent a part of these holdings.

ETFs

An exchange-traded fund is a type of investment fund that is traded on stock exchanges. ETFs are similar in many ways to mutual funds, except that ETFs are bought and sold throughout the day on stock exchanges, while mutual funds are bought and sold based on their price at day's end.

The S&P 500

For Beginner Investors

Many people don't know that the stock market is actually made up of many indexes or portfolios of stocks that are tied together. The three most popular indexes are the Dow Jones Industrial Average, Standard & Poors 500 (S&P 500), and the Nasdaq exchange. The Dow Jones represents the 30 largest companies in the United States. S&P 500 represents 500 of the largest companies from around the world. The Nasdaq exchange is a little more complicated, but it is typically seen as an indicator of the current strength of the tech sector. But which index is right for you and your first investments?

My recommendation is to start with the S&P 500. In most indexes, you purchase stock in an individual company. This means you have to do a lot of research to find —companies that are making money now and try to determine are they going to continue to make money? Even after you have purchased the stock, you have to monitor that company. Did they just have a bad article written about them that could lower their stock prices? Should you sell right now? Should you stay in and try to weather the storm? By investing in a broad perspective of stocks within the S&P 500, you are creating diversification that helps solve those problems and reduces the risk of investing.

Real Estate

Many people choose real estate as their preferred way of building a passive income. With real estate, if you do not have cash, you can borrow most of the money, except the down payment, from a lender. The goal is to find a property that you purchase and then are able to get a monthly profit from after the mortgage and expenses have been paid. The tenant who leases the property pays off the mortgage and ideally any of the expenses.

Three ways to earn money from real estate:
1. Cash flow
2. Property appreciation
3. Balance being paid off

Following is an example of a successful residential property investment where you make money from the bank's money:

- Let's say you borrow $100,000 for a house
- Your monthly mortgage payment is $800
- You charge a tenant $1,150 rent each month
- Giving you a $350 monthly profit
- $350 x 12 = $4,200 annual profit

- $4,200 x 10 = $42,000 profit over 10 years
- $10,000 of appreciation in 10 years.
- $10,000 reduction in balance paid down by the tenant
- $10,000 appreciation + $10,000 principal reduction+ $42,000 monthly profit
- Total of +$62,000 of cash and equity in 10 years.

Once the tenant pays the mortgage completely off, you will have a much larger profit.

How many times can you do this? As many times as you like. Remember, the bank's main source of revenue is the interest they charge for the money they loan. Keep a high credit score, and you will be a preferred customer.

Prepare for Retirement

Life is energy! When you sleep, you burn about 600 calories for the lungs to pump, the heart to beat, and all the other regulatory functions that happen involuntarily for life to continue. To cut the grass, you are using energy. To earn a living, you are trading energy. We do not know how much energy we will be allotted. We do know that if we live a long time, our energy capacity will be diminished. There will likely be a time you will not have the energy required to earn a living. Save and prepare for when this time comes. You would be wise to have the house paid off, zero debt, and a retirement account that you have properly funded so you can live for 20 to 30 years without using energy to earn a living. The most popular ways to do that today is to participate in your 401(k) retirement program or individual retirement account. The government knows that social security will not be enough for you to live on and will exempt the money set aside for retirement from taxes. Also, this money will grow tax-free until you retire. Many companies will also match your contributions up to a certain percentage. Getting started early and properly funding your retirement is one of the best financial decisions you can make so you can still enjoy life after you stop trading energy for money.

Conclusion

Make sure that you do everything you can to educate yourself about your finances. Remember, as you work to establish financial freedom you want to make your money work for you, not the other way around. The more you make your money work for you, the less you will have to trade energy for money.

STEP 6

Understanding Insurance

Insurance, like death and taxes, is an inescapable part of life. It can also be a very confusing part of life. In order to understand how insurance works, it is first important to understand what exactly insurance is.

Like many, your first thought is probably to head over to Google and do a quick search for the definition of insurance. Even a cursory search online will bring up several different definitions of insurance, many of them that will leave your head spinning. Do not panic; let's first look at a simple definition of insurance.

- Insurance is protection from a loss.

Ok, that definition might also be a little complicated. So, let's break it down a little more. **Often in life we may incur high out-of-pocket costs. Insurance is used to either repay us from these costs or to reduce them overall.**

Now that we have a working definition, the next question is, how does insurance work? Probably the most common type of insurance you will use is Auto Insurance. Nearly everywhere you operate a vehicle requires by law that you have insurance on the vehicle. The first thing you should do is identify the risk—what could happen that would cause you to use insurance.

- Getting into a car accident

Now you know the risk factor of —a car accident. But what about the loss? What could happen with a car accident that requires you to pay out-of-pocket?

- Pay to repair or replace your car
- Pay to repair or replace someone else's car
- Pay to repair someone's personal property
- Bills for personal injuries obtained during an accident
- Bills for other people's injuries obtained during an accident

These can become very expensive, very quickly. The cost of repairing or replacing a vehicle can be thousands of dollars. Even more scary, medical costs associated with car accidents can soar into the tens of thousands of dollars! How do you prevent having to pay all of that money out of pocket? By having a car insurance policy.

There is a very important caveat to insurance; you need to have purchased the policy BEFORE you get into a car accident. Today this can be done by answering a series of questions online before sending you an initial payment. Continuing with our example of car insurance, what do you need to get a policy?

One of the biggest things an insurance company is going to want is your driving record. Have you been in any accidents previously? What about tickets from the police? Have you been driving for six months or six years? All of these questions help them generate a risk model that will tell the company what the chances are you will get into an accident. The higher your chances of getting into an accident, the higher your premium will be. Therefore, it is important to practice safe driving. The safer you drive, the less money it will cost you.

They will need to know the detailed conditions of the car you want to insure. These often include the year it was made, how many miles it has, has it been involved in any accidents and if so how many. Now, you may ask, why do they care what condition my vehicle is in? Let's look at an example.

The insurance company will take all the information you give them about your vehicle and use information from other people that have similar vehicles. They will feed this into an algorithm that will tell them what the vehicle is worth. Note, sometimes the vehicle might be worth more or less than what you paid for it. So, let's say the insurance company determines that your vehicle is worth ten thousand dollars.

Based on that car value, you will now choose your coverage limits. You use this to choose your coverage limits . Many places have laws that will require you to purchase a minimum amount of coverage. There are three main coverage limits that you can select—per-person injury, per accident, and property damage. This determines how much the insurance company is liable for, and the higher your coverage limits, the higher your premium is going to be.

That's the second time that we've mentioned your premium. What is that? When you complete the process of applying for insurance, you will usually be given a six-month premium. This is how much it will cost you for six months of insurance on your vehicle. There are several ways to pay this premium; you can pay monthly, bi-monthly, or the whole six months all at once. Many companies will offer you discounts if you pay for the whole six months at once. Every six months, your insurance is automatically renewed unless you make changes or cancel it.

Oh no! You got into an accident, and the entire front of your vehicle has been destroyed! What do you do now?

First, you want to make sure everyone involved in the accident is ok and call the police. No matter how big or small the accident, no matter who is at fault, you must always call the police and request a police report. Your insurance will use that report to determine who was at fault for the accident. It also serves as a protection for you should someone make an accusation against you at a later date.

After determining that everyone is safe and the police have been called, you need to call your insurance. You will file a claim with your insurance company right away. This claim gets the ball rolling on having your vehicle fixed and back on the road. Many times, your insurance company will help get your vehicle to a body shop with whom they have a relationship.

The insurance company will send out an appraiser to determine how much it will cost to repair your car. This estimate will then be compared to the value of your vehicle. If it's going to cost twelve thousand dollars to repair your vehicle, but your vehicle is only worth ten thousand, it makes little sense for them to pay that extra two thousand dollars.

This is where, depending on your insurance policy, there are typically two different options. The first option is the insurance company will replace the vehicle for you. This means they will work to find another vehicle similar in age, style, and features to replace the one that was destroyed. The other option is a check for the determined insurance value of your vehicle. This is referred to as the replacement cost by the insurance company. If it is cheaper to replace the vehicle than to repair it, they will choose to replace it.

But what if it's only going to cost one thousand dollars to repair your vehicle? Then the cheaper option for the insurance company will be to repair your current vehicle. Now there is another wrinkle to the process; you are going to have to pay a deductible. The deductible is how much you have to pay out of pocket before the insurance will pick up the rest of the cost.

Many of the same factors that were used to determine your premium will also determine how much your deductible will be. You can often select your deductible, paying more every month for a lower deductible or less every month for a higher one. There are also insurance companies that may offer reduced deductibles based on how long you go without having a claim, some even reducing the deductible to zero.

Once you have paid your deductible, your insurance will cover the rest of the cost to repair your vehicle. Another benefit of having insurance is that they usually have working relationships with local body shops. This helps get the repair work done quickly and helps ensure excellent quality as well. Finally, after this entire process is complete, you will get your vehicle (or a new one) back in working order.

This is a general overlook of how insurance works. Let's take a brief look at some of the other insurance you will probably encounter.

Health Insurance: Health insurance is very important as it covers a wide multitude of things. Doctor's visits, medication, and even surgeries are covered by health insurance. Most people get their health insurance through their employer, who will pay part of the premium. The rest of the premium is deducted from every paycheck. Finally, instead of paying a deductible, health insurance uses copayments, the rate of which depends on the service or medication being provided. Health insurance is important. If you or a loved one find themselves facing health issues, the cost can quickly spiral out of control. Having insurance will help mitigate those costs while making sure you or your loved one gets the best care available.

- Dental: Because of the high costs associated with it, dental insurance is typically not included with health insurance and requires a separate policy. Dental insurance is typically purchased through an employer, similar to health insurance.

- Vision: Just like dental insurance, vision insurance is not included in general health insurance and requires a separate policy. It is also purchased through your employer.

- e.g. e coverageassociated .Homeowners: Homeowners insurance is required by mortgage companies and is also very good to have. It protects your home and the contents inside from damage, theft, and even acts of nature. Depending on where you live, you may be required to have specific riders attached to your homeowner's insurance, like flood, fire, or even tornado.

- Renters: Renter's insurance operates similar to homeowner's insurance, but for people who rent a house or an apartment. While it rarely protects the actual building, it will protect your personal property inside the rental property.

Another very important example of insurance that you should have is life insurance. We all wish that we could live forever, but the sad truth is that we can't. When we pass away, it's important to make sure that our loved ones are not left with a financial burden. This burden can include the costs of the funeral, paying off debt, and even loss of income to a family. Having health insurance will help your loved ones with the financial struggles during such a trying time.

There is another caveat to insurance, how much it costs. Almost all insurance policies are based on risk. As mentioned earlier, if you are at a higher risk of getting into an accident, your auto insurance premium will be higher. The same goes for life insurance. If you smoke or drink too much, your risk is higher, and therefore it will cost you more.

There is another misunderstanding of life insurance. Many people think that when you are young, you don't need life insurance. But there are two big issues with this train of thought. The first being that an accident can happen at any time, no matter what your age is. The second is that the older you get, the higher your risk of using the insurance. If you wait to get life insurance, your premium will be higher than if you get it when you are younger. This isn't to say that you need to run out and get life insurance right now. But it's an important thing to think about as you transition into being an adult.

As has been mentioned before, there are many cases when you are required to purchase insurance. If you own and operate a vehicle, you will be required by law to have insurance. If you own a home and pay a monthly mortgage, the mortgage company will require you to have an insurance policy.

While insurance is very complicated, it is not impossible to understand. This chapter gives you a good overview of how insurance works. But, when you are shopping for your own insurance, you need to take the time to research the policy you are purchasing. They are all different and have different benefits. At the end of the day, the peace of mind offered by insurance outweighs the cost.

Conclusion

Understanding is Powerful!

I am older, mature, and humble. I have made my share of mistakes and have had my share of failures. Failure is a part of the success plan. Try to keep that part small, but don't fear failure. I believe in doing the hard stuff. My favorite quote is, "Everyone can do it when it is easy. Only a few can do it when it is hard." Be a lifelong learner. Because I have intentionally sought knowledge and wisdom there are decisions I made when I was younger that I would not make today. Be smart enough to know that you can be wrong. Seek council; get a mentor. Mentors will help you see wider, farther, and quicker. Remember your attitude will make more of a difference than your education and experience. Invest in your personal growth as well. Sometimes we get stuck and need motivation, support, and accountability—hire a coach. Life has periods of wilderness—hire a professional therapist and feed your spirit daily!

Time is your greatest asset because it is not renewable. Once it is gone, it is gone. Use it wisely. Health is difficult to restore once it has been compromised. Time with poor health is hell. Relationships are what we live for. We all desire connection with people who are important to us. Do not allow your drive for more money to *reduce* your time, health, and relationships!

I have always loved learning and searching for understanding. and knowledge as well as I have a passion for teaching and encouraging people to reach for their goals. I regularly teach personal growth, fitness, and financial workshops. For more information, visit the website: www.michaelbootcampthomas.com.

Made in the USA
Las Vegas, NV
06 December 2022

61298069R00037